Christina the Astonishing

Jane Draycott's collections include, from Two Rivers Press, *Tideway* (2002, reissued 2022), poems about the lives of the watermen and women working on the London Thames, and *Storms Under the Skin* (2017) translations from the poems of artist-writer Henri Michaux, as well as five collections from Carcanet Press, including *The Occupant* (2016, Poetry Book Society Recommendation), *Over* (2009, T S Eliot Prize shortlist) and her prize-winning translation of the 14th-century dream-elegy *Pearl*. She teaches on postgraduate writing programmes at the universities of Oxford and Lancaster and is a Fellow of the Royal Society of Literature.

Lesley Saunders is the author of several poetry collections, most recently *This Thing of Blood & Love* (Two Rivers Press 2022) and, with artist Rebecca Swainston, *Days of Wonder* (Hippocrates Press 2021), a document of the Covid-19 pandemic. Her English translations – including the poem that won the 2016 Stephen Spender award – of renowned Portuguese poet Maria Teresa Horta were published as *Point of Honour* (Two Rivers Press 2019). Lesley works on collaborative projects with visual artists, sculptors, musicians, photographers and dancers as well as other poets. Otherwise, she is a visiting professor at UCL Institute of Education, London, and an honorary research fellow at Oxford University Department of Education.

Also by Two Rivers Poets

David Attwooll, *The Sound Ladder* (2015)
Charles Baudelaire, *Paris Scenes* translated by Ian Brinton (2021)
William Bedford, *The Dancers of Colbek* (2020)
Kate Behrens, *Man with Bombe Alaska* (2016)
Kate Behrens, *Penumbra* (2019)
Kate Behrens, *Transitional Spaces* (2022)
Conor Carville, *English Martyrs* (2019)
David Cooke, *A Murmuration* (2015)
David Cooke, *Sicilian Elephants* (2021)
Tim Dooley, *Discoveries* (2022)
Jane Draycott, *Tideway* (re-issued 2022)
Claire Dyer, *Interference Effects* (2016)
Claire Dyer, *Yield* (2021)
John Froy, *Sandpaper & Seahorses* (2018)
James Harpur, *The Examined Life* (2021)
Maria Teresa Horta, *Point of Honour* translated by Lesley Saunders (2019)
Ian House, *Just a Moment* (2020)
Rosie Jackson & Graham Burchell, *Two Girls and a Beehive* (2020)
Gill Learner, *Chill Factor* (2016)
Gill Learner, *Change* (2021)
Sue Leigh, *Chosen Hill* (2018)
Sue Leigh, *Her Orchards* (2021)
Becci Louise, *Octopus Medicine* (2017)
Mairi MacInnes, *Amazing Memories of Childhood, etc.* (2016)
Steven Matthews, *On Magnetism* (2017)
Henri Michaux, *Storms under the Skin* translated by Jane Draycott (2017)
René Noyau, *Earth on Fire and other Poems* translated by Gérard Noyau with Peter Pegnall (2021)
James Peake, *Reaction Time of Glass* (2019)
James Peake, *The Star in the Branches* (2022)
Peter Robinson & David Inshaw, *Bonjour Mr Inshaw* (2020)
Peter Robinson, *English Nettles* (re-issued 2022)
Lesley Saunders, *Nominy-Dominy* (2018)
Lesley Saunders, *This Thing of Blood & Love* (2022)
Jack Thacker, *Handling* (2018)
Susan Utting, *Half the Human Race* (2017)
Jean Watkins, *Precarious Lives* (2018)

Christina
the Astonishing

Jane Draycott & Lesley Saunders

Artwork by Peter Hay

First published in the UK in 1998 by Two Rivers Press
Second edition published 2022
7 Denmark Road, Reading RG1 5PA.
www.tworiverspress.com

© in poems Jane Draycott & Lesley Saunders 1998
© in artwork Peter Hay 1998

The right of the poets to be identified as the authors of this work
has been asserted by them in accordance with the Copyright, Designs
and Patents Act of 1988.

All rights reserved. No part of this publication may be reproduced,
stored in or introduced into a retrieval system, or transmitted,
in any form, or by any means (electronic, mechanical, photocopying,
recording or otherwise) without the prior written permission
of the publisher.

ISBN 978-1-915048-00-4

1 2 3 4 5 6 7 8 9

Two Rivers Press is represented in the UK by Inpress Ltd
and distributed by Ingram Publisher Services UK.

Cover design by Nadja Guggi with a lithograph by Peter Hay
Text design by Nadja Guggi and typeset in Janson and Parisine

Printed and bound in Great Britain by Severn, Gloucester

Acknowledgements

Thanks are due to the editors of the *Exeter Anthology 1997*, *Poetry London Newsletter* and *The Rialto* in which some of these poems first appeared. Thanks are also due to BBC Radio 4's *A Good Read*, in which *Christina the Astonishing* was reviewed, hosted by Sarah LeFanu and first broadcast on 31 August 1999 (re-broadcast 2015).

Acknowledgements are due to Caroline Walker Bynum, for *Holy Feast, Holy Fast: The Religious Significance of Food to Mediaeval Women* (University of California Press 1987); and to Marina Warner, for several articles published in *The London Review of Books*.

The authors would like to express our personal gratitude to Ludwig Vandenhove (mayor of Sint-Truiden), Danny Gennez (guide and companion) and Kamiel Stevaux (local historian) for their generous hospitality, practical help and insights into Christina's life, locality and times. We should also like to thank Norman Price and Malcolm Rigg for their technical expertise (and companionship) in capturing the journey we made to Belgium on tape and camera in summer 1996.

The collection itself and many individual poems in it benefited immeasurably from the editing skills of Philip Gross, whose incisive comments and critical suggestions always respected the dreamlike logic of poetic process. Thanks are due to Keiren Phelan, then Literature Officer at Southern Arts, for making a grant available to assist with the work.

We also want to record how much we valued working with Peter Hay, as editor, publisher and artist: his understandings of Christina's life and significance through a stream of visual images – reproduced here from original hand-coloured lithographs kindly supplied by various friends and patrons – stimulated us to re-imagine things we thought we knew and to look again at the unconscious motifs we had somehow chosen to represent her.

Finally, we would like to thank Peter Robinson, Barbara Morris and Nadja Guggi for all their work to make this new edition possible.

Contents

Introduction | xii

Christina the Astonishing

To the Church, from Christina | 1
Lesley Saunders

'An emaciated body will more readily pass the narrow gate...' | 2
Tertullian, Church Father (2nd-c.CE)

The girlhood of St Christina | 3
Jane Draycott

Hunger, Christ god, and thirst for sight of you | 4
Radbod, Bishop of Utrecht (10th-c.CE)

Gifts | 6
Lesley Saunders

See the god-Christ | 8
Paulinus of Nola, scholar (5th-c.CE)

Concerning women's vices | 9
Burchard, Bishop of Worms (10th-c.CE)

Soul food | 11
Lesley Saunders

Acta Sanctorum 1, 5 | 13

The levitation of St Christina | 14
Jane Draycott

'Undoubtedly some of the marvels...' | 15
Herbert Thurston (1922)

What she can't take | 16
Jane Draycott

Here they come, the virtuous virgins | 18
Siegebert of Gembloux, historian (10th-c.CE)

The language of flowers | 19
Lesley Saunders

Acta Sanctorum 1, 11 | 21

Daughter my dove | 22
Lesley Saunders

Love's violence grazes me | 24
Carmina Burana *(13th-c.CE)*

What the baker-woman saw | 25
Jane Draycott

'Lay people were typically required to memorise…' | 27
J. Shinners (1997)

Tongues | 28
Lesley Saunders

Acta Sanctorum 2, 15 | 31

Up here | 32
Jane Draycott

Futurist | 34
Lesley Saunders

'Most mediaeval people differed from most of us today…' | 36
R.E. Lerner (1983)

Acta Sanctorum 3, 32 | 37

From Christina's sister to her husband | 40
Lesley Saunders

To Christina from her sister | 41
Lesley Saunders

Salvation as a diving-suit | 43
Jane Draycott

What goes around | 44
Lesley Saunders

How Saint Christina sang | 45
Lesley Saunders

The cave | 47
Jane Draycott

When I woke, the darkest dreams continued…
I was forced to travel | 49
Jane Draycott

Acta Sanctorum 4, 38 | 50

Virgin | 51
Lesley Saunders

Letter from Hadewijch | 53
Hadewijch of Brabant (13th-c.CE)

What the poet said | 54
Lesley Saunders

'Beside this vertigo of stone…' | 56
Jane Draycott

'We shall have no clouds today…' | 57
Jane Draycott

'The mountain is paralysed…' | 59
Jane Draycott

'Take it or leave it…' | 60
Jane Draycott

'Alone in night's wide bed…' | 61
Jane Draycott

'The last years of her life…' | 61
A. Butler, Lives of the Saints *(1756–9)*

She settles down after her miraculous time as a bird | 62
Lesley Saunders

From the Prioress' journal | 64
Jane Draycott

The visit | 65
Lesley Saunders

Acta Sanctorum 5, 52 | 67

The tunnel | 68
Jane Draycott

'Christina died in the convent in 1224…' | 69
Danny Gennez (1996)

Relic | 70
Jane Draycott

And will our daughters fly? | 71
Lesley Saunders

References | 74

All translations from the Latin are by Lesley Saunders, except where otherwise stated.

For Sophie, Holly and Laura

'there is little in the recorded history of Christina of Brusthem to make us think she was other than a pathological case.'
—*Butler's Lives of the Saints*

'She was one of the strongest women in the Middle Ages. Now we would say she was an emancipated woman.'
—Polly Vanmarsenille
　Custodian, Church of the Holy Virgin, Sint-Truiden

Introduction

This book came into being over three years of poetic collaboration as the two of us, having quite by chance turned up a brief reference to the 12th-century mystic Christina Mirabilis – Christina the Astonishing – delved deeper and deeper into contemporary and modern meanings of her life.

James Bentley's 1986 *Calendar of Saints* tells her story in summary:

> 'Christina the Astonishing was born in Belgium, at Brusthem near Liège, in the year 1150. By the time she was fifteen she and her two elder sisters were orphans. Her first extraordinary piece of behaviour happened after she had suffered some sort of fit, so that she fell deeply unconscious and seemed quite dead. A requiem Mass was being said for the saint's soul when she suddenly rose from her open coffin and sped up into the rafters of the church. Only her elder sister had the presence of mind not to run away in fright.
>
> Thenceforth the saint continued to behave as one of the great eccentrics of Christendom. She dressed in rags bound together with saplings. She liked being swung round and round mill wheels and seemed never to get hurt doing so. To escape the smell of humans she would frequently hide inside ovens. At a church in a place called Wellen she climbed into the large font and sat in the water.
>
> Yet many people came to her for good advice. In her later years she settled in a convent at Saint-Trond [Sint-Truiden in Flemish], and there many came to seek her counsel.'

More details of Christina's life and works can be found in her biography, *Vita S. Christinae Mirabilis Virginis* written by the Dominican biographer Thomas de Chantimpré in 1232 (reproduced in the *Acta Sanctorum* – see References), on the basis of an account by her contemporary Cardinal Jacques de Vitry. De Chantimpré wrote his biography of Christina more than forty years after the events which in his narrative seem so incredible. As the 20th-century Catholic scholar Fr. Herbert Thurston noted, de Chantimpré was himself 'all agape for miracles and the most uncritical of chroniclers.' However, his is the only discursive source we have.

De Chantimpré says that Christina came from a farming family, that she was essentially an illiterate peasant girl. But already by her adolescence she had acquired a reputation – and not altogether a positive one – for her extreme religious devotion, fasting and capacity for mystical experience. She came by the epithet 'Mirabilis' (Astonishing) both because of the remarkable events or miracles surrounding her life and, it would seem, her own extraordinary behaviour.

Was Christina a 'pathological case', as Alban Butler claimed in his *Lives of the Saints*? Well, she was no*t* alone. There were many women living through the extraordinary upheavals of the twelfth and thirteenth centuries in Europe who were transgressive with regard to both religious orthodoxy and conventions of female behaviour. They had a passion for the divine and a calling to model their lives on Christ's corporeal suffering (a form of *imitatio Christi*), rather than on the maternal anguish of the Virgin Mary. They were not able or willing to become nuns, whose entry into convent life would be financed and supported by well-off families, but instead lived their devotional lives alone and outside the established order.

Moreover, the image of the female self as food, the conflict between devouring and (self-)denial, was a central aspect of this kind of feminine religious activity, as Caroline Walker Bynum so vividly relates. We could not hope to understand Christina simply from the viewpoint of the late 20th century: with hindsight, it is as if we were trying to construct a pre-Freudian account of the relationship between the female body and spirit that attempted to be true to her lived experience.

In the summer of 1996 we made a kind of pilgrimage together to Christina's birthplace in the village of Brusthem and other places known to her, including the church where she first 'died' in the nearby town of Sint-Truiden. We were hosted on a tour of the town by the extremely generous municipal guide Danny Genez, with his great store of knowledge about the many local legends attached to Christina's life and death. It turned out to be a weekend of surprise and serendipity:

by lucky coincidence, as we walked through the village of Brusthem, we came across local historian Kamiel Stevaux passing by on his bike. He in turn recruited the kind offices of the local priest's housekeeper as impromptu interpreter for a whole host of further intriguing anecdotes about Christina.

When it came to writing the poems, therefore, we found there was no single 'truth' to be uncovered. We needed to be able to see Christina from many different, even contradictory, angles. Thomas de Chantimpré tells us 'The last years of her life Christina passed in the convent of Sint-Truiden, and there she died at the age of seventy-four. While she was living there, many nobles came to seek her advice.' Isn't it interesting, and a great puzzle, that Christina's life started in wildness and ended in wisdom? What she was known for in her youth was flying, being flighty; yet what brought her fame as an old woman was her advice to the powerful.

It is tempting to see in Christina's story the logic, the trajectory, of what might be a peculiarly female journey through life, unplanned and unpredictable. But the many resonances of her story are even more richly complex than that. In this book we have tried to tell or retell Christina's story, while also finding that we wanted to make poems in response to ideas or feelings she called up in us both, and which were quite personal to each of us. So Lesley's closing poem from our close-knit collaboration 'And will our daughters fly?' is dedicated, like the book as a whole, to the three daughters we have between us.

> Jane Draycott & Lesley Saunders,
> November 2021

Christina the Astonishing

To the Church, from Christina

found a seed
at the heart
of the morning.
I scooped its flesh
with a bone spoon
then swallowed the stone.
Finches flew
out of my stiff arms.
I sprouted a thousand hands.
My blood ran green and sweet.
I am bursting with strangeness.
You fell me for a lintel.

I found an ear of rye
which I split with a flint knife.
I chewed the grains.
By nightfall I was a field
on the auburn earth.
Crickets whirred in my hair.
A month's sun bleaches me
from sea-green to silver.
You mill me for flour.

I found a syllable
under the wind's tongue.
It crept in my ear.
I am an exhalation of dialects,
I weep an alphabet of brooks.
You bind me in a book.

An emaciated body will more readily pass the narrow gate [of paradise], a light body will resurrect more rapidly, and in the grave a wasted body will be preserved best.

— Tertullian, Church Father (2nd-c.CE)

The girlhood of St Christina

Christ, let me be your fasting-girl,
feasting on tears. Let me drink you in the rain
you trickle down the insides of my skin
and in the sweet cold weepings of these walls.

My sisters eat like apes – I am their torment
and give to strangers passing on the road.
Chained here in the dark my song flies upward:
Lord, like the angels, let me be transparent.

In the dream I am famous: Christ's only daughter
and maker of eye-white pots. I meet a beggar
and his child drinking from thimbles in the desert.
My weeping fills their bowls with guilty water.

Lord let me be your ragamuffin, suffering for years
before I'm queen. Let me dance the dying swan
for you, my pas de deux perfected and danced alone
with you. O lord, let it always end in tears.

Hunger, Christ god, and thirst for sight of you

hunger, Christ god, and thirst for sight of you
    have stopped me eating fleshly food –
give yourself to be devoured and drunk, salvation's drink,
you be the only meal for the unknown way

and when long fasting has famished the world wanderer
gorge him, likeness of our father, on your gaze

aesuries te, Christe deus, sitis atque vivendi
iam modo carnales me vetat esse dapes.
da modo te vesci, te potum haurire salutis;
unicus ignote tu cybus esto vie.
et quem longa fames errantem ambesit in orbe,
nunc satia vultu, patris imago, tuo.

—Radbod, Bishop of Utrecht (10th-c.CE)

Gifts

'Christina the Astonishing came from a family so poor
that she had nothing to give up except food and drink'
—Caroline Walker Bynum

Oh Jesus now she's giving away the family bread!
She's emptied the cupboards, dumped everything in an old bucket,
then ran into the road and grabbed people – Berthe and
Agnes on their way to market, the Leeuwardens,
even fat old Jehan – begging them
to take the sorrel, the wormy apples,
the thin meat, shrieking like a stuck pig
Here, yes, take it, you must eat.

She must give it away
oh all of it even the grey
dough that's still proving
so as not to turn into
so as to not to taste
the stretched and freckled
flesh of, the muscle and gristle
and mucilage and curds of –

craving only
the thinnest shavings
of the flayed god
pale as parchment
the secret word that passes
through closed lips.

She eats nothing, needs nothing, oozes sanctity.
Humanity stinks, according to Her Holiness.
All her furniture's in the yard, chucked
through the window, smashed. Her sisters try
to knock some sense into her – her tears gush
thick as beeswax, ambergris, that expensive
ointment the apothecary sells.

Crying with hunger, they haul her to her room.
Who does she think she is?
In this small desert she unties her scarf, scrapes
her fingers over bony breasts, willing
the dew to weep from them

fine as Saint Joseph's breath
sweet as virgins' tears that can move
the far spheres of the stars with love
or keep this flesh from its own rot –

oh how hard she strains to undo
her body
to swallow this sea, this welter
of longing
to be the Christina that feeds
her God

See the god-Christ

see the god-Christ wrapped in our body's veil
who as flesh is frail, as word is bread, as cross is grief:

how hard a shell it needs, to keep Christ's heavenly heart
shut up in flesh, this cross that speaks, that feeds us…

cerne deum nostro velatum corpore Christum,
qui fragile carne est, verbo cibus et cruce amarus:
dura superficies, verbum crucis et crucis esca est,
coelestem Christi claudens in carne medullam…

— Paulinus of Nola, scholar (5th-c.CE)

Concerning women's vices

Have you done what some women are wont to do? They take a live fish and put it in their vagina, keeping it there for a while until it is dead. Then they cook it or roast it and give it to their husbands to eat, doing this in order to make the men be more ardent in their love for them. If you have, you should do two years of penance on the appointed fast days.

Have you done what some women are accustomed to do? They lie face down on the ground, uncover their buttocks, and tell someone to make bread on their naked buttocks. When they have cooked it, they give it to their husbands to eat. They do this in order to make them more ardent in their love for them. If you have, you should do two years of penance on the appointed fast days.

Have you done what some women are accustomed to do? They take off their clothes and smear honey all over their naked body. With the honey on their body they roll themselves back and forth over wheat on a sheet spread on the ground. They carefully collect all the grains of wheat sticking to their moist body, put them in a mill, turn the mill in the opposite direction of the sun, grind the wheat into flour, and bake bread from it. Then they serve it to their husbands to eat, who then grow weak and die. If you have, you should do penance for forty days on bread and water.

—Burchard, Bishop of Worms (10th-c.CE)

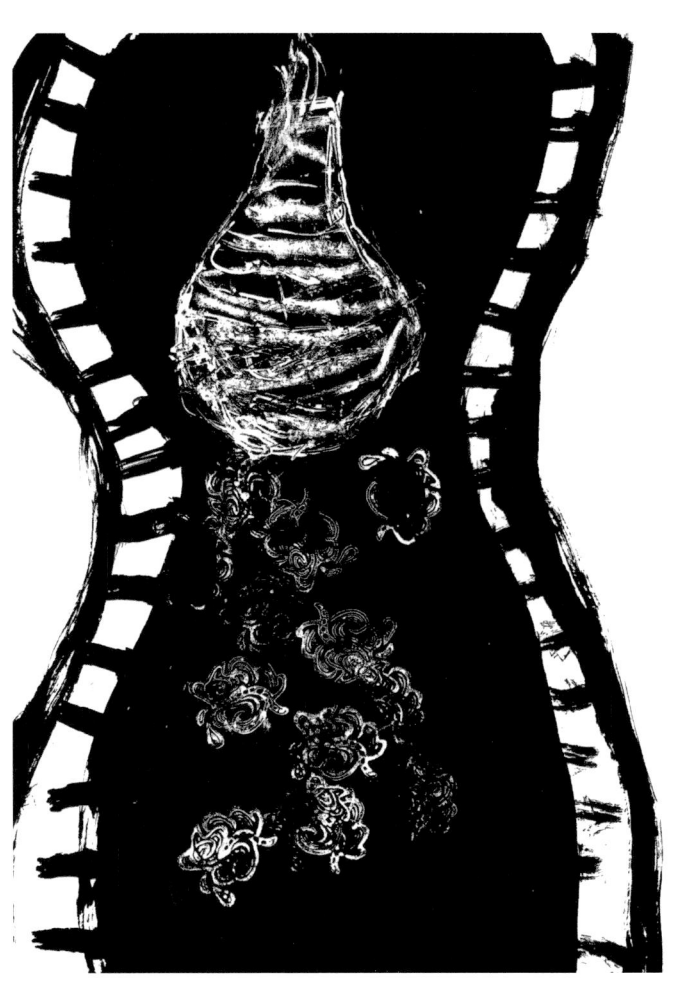

Soul food

'In the 17th century … the general opinion of herbalists
and botanists and connoisseurs of simples was that
the banana was the strongest candidate for the original
tree of the knowledge of good and evil.'
—Marina Warner

You are what you eat. You eat
what you are not, handing into your body
licit and illicit goods, additives
of anger and grief, carbohydrates
of easy-come easy-go comfort,
concise histories of continents and beliefs.
Living off the fat of many lands
I can eat yams in a cold climate,
sweet potato, guava, banana:

knowledge of good and not-good.
One soft-scented huge-budded flower
makes enough thick-fingered fruit
to weigh a woman with. Perhaps you think
of her as your breast your fig your flesh
who wove you skirts of leaves, held parliament
with snakes on your behalf. You
misconstrue me if you think I feel more
than I think or find feeling more
congenial than thought. I am hungry
for meaning. Being food,

I know there's energy in the freshly
killed body that feeds the spirit directly, it's
in the sigh of fleeing yeast, the spurt
of sweet juice. I remember my tall son's
infant anus flowering with shit the colour
of mangos. Don't you think a man

should be judged by how well he dresses
the gracious leaves of a salad
with the vinegar, oil and salt of him?

But yes, bite me with your words.
Let me feel your soul (said
the beguine) slip down my throat
like a fish.

While the sacrifice of the Mass was being offered at her funeral, suddenly the body shivered and stood up from the bier, and straightway rising into the air like a bird she flew up to the rafters of the building. All the company present took flight and only her elder sister remained, trembling, until Mass was over, whereupon the other was constrained by the priest with the Blessed Sacrament to descend to earth again. It was the subtlety of her spiritual substance, so some conjecture, which left a loathing for the odour proceeding from the bodies of men.

Cumque pro depositione eius Missarum oblatio fieret subito commotum corpus exsurrexit in feretro, statimque instar avis evecta templi trabes ascendit. Fugientibus ergo cunctis qui aderant, sola soror aetate major cum timore remanist usque post Missam immobilis perseverans, a presbytero ecclesiae sacramento constricta, est coacta descendere: horrebat enim, ut quidam autumant, subtilitas eius spiritus odorem corporum humanorum.

—*Acta Sanctorum* [Acts of the Saints] 1, 5

The levitation of St Christina

I rise on a wing and a prayer. In the aisles Father Thomas
is singing his heart out O Lamb of God all shaven and shorn
and loud enough to waken the dead. Have mercy upon us.

Up here in the gods where anything goes I am Lucifer, born
like a swan from a box, striking the light and standing well clear
of the tears, of the tar and the feathers, and of the coffin's yawn

that takest away Father Thomas' face, that waning moon in the
   filthy air,
that gaping wound in the side of the world. And the O in his mouth
is the sins, is enough to make the angels weep. Receive our prayer.

Out of the hive of the yet to be born, I'm the queen bee, behemoth
in the candle's flame, shifting my shape in the smoke dance,
the dance of death, whose sting is a needle fixed on celestial north.

I leap, and my shadow's a shroud-span over the mountains,
   an icy stroke
down the cheek of the earth. I have only to touch the hills and
   they shall smoke.

Undoubtedly some of the marvels recounted of Christina have all the air of deliberate inventions due to the morbid imagination of an unscrupulous romancer. Such, for example, is the story that when the stench which she perceived to come from her fellow men had driven her into solitary places far from their abodes and when she in consequence was in danger of starvation, God miraculously caused her breasts to fill with milk upon which she supported herself for nine weeks. Equally preposterous are the assertions that … while during yet another period of imprisonment when her body owing to the tightness of her bonds was covered with sores her breasts became filled with a wonderful oil with which she healed her wounds and made the hard crusts given her for food delicious to the palate.

—Herbert Thurston, *The Month* (1922)

What she can't take

What she can't take
is in her face. Little Miss Muffet
and the spider of sweet surrender, its glittering
net to lay a body down on. She's risen
above all that.

We smell of cheese
she says. Junked up with things
we have eaten and do not remember. The list
is endless of the things she wouldn't give
a thank-you for:

the reek of myrrh
on a Saracen's skin, the love
on his fingers, *lachrymator terribilis*,
the wine-cave's velvet fungus, drunk
on the earth's dark life.

What she likes
is the moon, the way
it has no smell, can never rot
or turn its back or show
its other face.

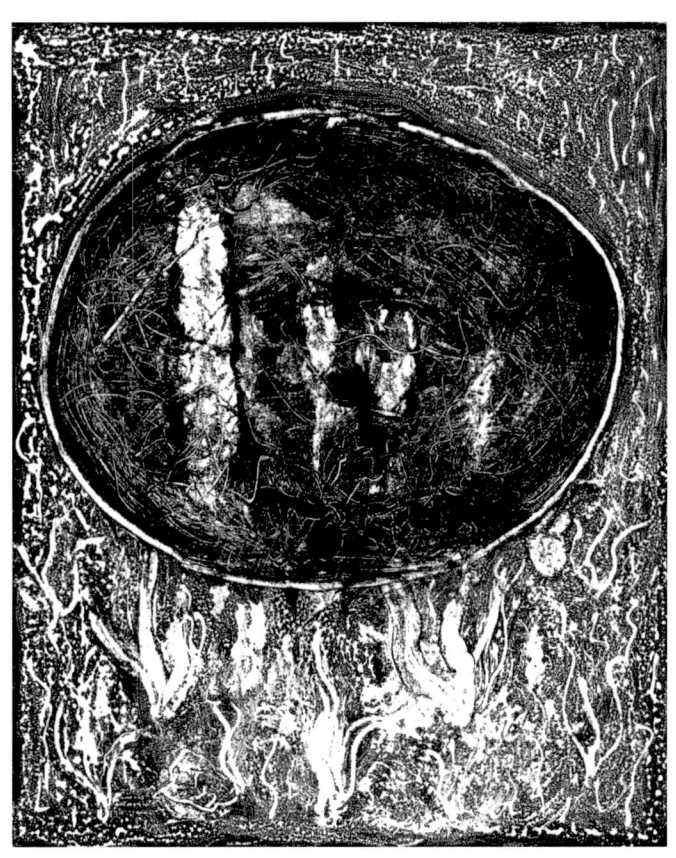

Here they come, the virtuous virgins

Here they come, the virtuous virgins, one after another,
Gertrudis, Agnes, Priscilla, Cecilia,
Lucia, Petronilla, Tecla, Agatha, Barbara, Juliana,
And many more whose names I never knew
or, knowing, did not give their due –
full of faith and pure of heart
they were fit to take God's part…

Now wandering in the wide green spaces
plaiting posies, gathering graces,
they fill their arms with the suffering rose,
love's violets and the lily of woes.

Hinc virginalis sancta frequentia
Gertrudis, Agnes, Prisca, Cecilia,
*   Lucia, Petronilla, Tecla,*
*   Agatha, Barbara, Juliana,*
Multaeque quarum nomina non lego
aut lecta nunc his addere negligo,
*   dignas Deo quas fecit esse*
*   et integritas animae fidesque…*
Hae pervagantes prata recentia
pro velle querunt serta decentia
*   rosas legentes passionis*
*   lilia vel violas amoris.*

— Siegebert of Gembloux, historian (10th-c.CE)

The language of flowers

the smell you gagged on
that caught in your throat
a catarrh of roses

a funeral of flowers so huge you'd
to think of Caesar and his
pavement of corpses

or the workers of Grasse treading petals
into perfume, rouging their skirts
bloodying the air

or these heavy heads of the rosa mundi
a corpus of crimson lolling in
the lap of the year.

She crept into fiery ovens where the bread was baking and there she suffered as any other mortal would suffer, so that her cries of anguish were terrible to hear; but when she made her way out again, no damage of any sort appeared in her body…

Ingrediebaturque clibanos ignivomos ad coquendum panes paratos, cruciebaturque incendiis velut aliquis nostrum, ita et horrifice clamaret prae angustia; nec tamen in egredientis corpore laesura forinsecus apparebat…

—*Acta Sanctorum* [Acts of the Saints] 1,11

Daughter my dove

What am I to you, daughter sweet maid?

This closet, where I fold away my face
snow-white and secret, waiting to be stained

And what am I to you, daughter my queen?

This hollow tree, this guilty beech
where I hang and heave like a fist of bees

But what am I to you, daughter beloved?

This oven, where I hide my stale flesh
and mourn all the yeast-demons which have fled

Then what am I to you, daughter my delight?

This coffin, where I kill time like a bride
impatient to be pricked with light, pure light

At last what am I to you, daughter my dove?

This house, whose skin fits like a glove
stitched from the daily corpses of love

Love's violence grazes me

Love's violence grazes me –
passion's anguish crazes me –
breathing fire, my breath is lost –
sweet mercy, unnail me from this cross…

dira vi amoris teror
et venereo axe vehor
igne ferventi suffocatus –
deme, pia, cruciatus

—*Carmina Burana* (13th-c.CE)

What the baker-woman saw

i
Crouched out of the wind behind the only rise
for miles, he has lit the first fire of the day:
Agni, god of braziers, beacons and the mackerel sky.

Between darkness and the scorched hands
of the morning, the windmill racks and turns
black, red, black, and breaks the backs of the wheat.

In the hanging fields, the shadows
measure their length. It is the third day.
You are there, down on your knees. It is all one now.

ii
I am the bread fantastical   the breath and the life
creator, destroyer   the loaf and the knife
I'm the cause and effect   the brick and the mortar
in sickness and health   the flour and the water
I'm tenant and landlord   pleasure and pain
lift me up lay me down   I'm the hills and the plains
agnus dei or Agni   the bend in the road
I'm nothing you don't have already   I am the Lord
but I'm not in the fire   I'm the still, I'm the small
I'm the voice that you hear in the oven   that's all.

iii
Midsummer's eve in a Flanders field,
the sky bellied out with heat. One
after another the pregnant women leap
across the bonfire of apple branches,
praying for their easy delivery. One way
or another, a life hereafter. The flames kick
inside the wild bells of their skirts.

Watching from the orchard, you are
your own new child. Phoenix and fire,
feeding on air and the transforming power
of pain. Night's edge creeps in at your feet,
grey, still warm. You and your child, out
lost in the woods. Soon you will climb together
into the long hot oven of tomorrow.

Lay people were typically required to memorise the brief Latin of the Lord's Prayer, Hail Mary and the Creed, though few would understand what they were saying without a vernacular translation. The word 'patter', for instance, derives from the rapidly moving lips of someone mechanically reciting the Paternoster… [This] prayer was such a part of ordinary life that it was commonly used to measure intervals of time; it is not unusual, for example, to find mediaeval recipes containing instructions to stir a dish 'for as long as it takes to say the Our Father'.

—J. Shinners, *Medieval Popular Religion* (1997)

Tongues

'She sang with astonishing sweetness in Latin which was clear as a bell and brilliantly ornamented with rhetorical devices… despite her lifelong ignorance of reading and writing'
—Thomas de Chantimpré

i
O dulcis gustus in pectoribus
et infusio cordium
in bono odore virtutum
My body has mouths
all of them hungry
for the confection
of words
I shall eat
my words
your words
stick
in my throat
but will never
hurt me nor
butter my parsnips

ii
In principio
was
the verbum
– not the
dumb dark
of boiling
Ocean,
not the
semaphores
of infinitesimal
amoebae,
not the

between-teeth
hiss of a
thunderbolt
puncturing the
first neutron
the nano-
second
before it
split –
just a
word,
a stutter
on the
galactic
wireless

iii
A verb is a doing word.
What did the verb-word do?
What it did was god
but we didn't get it
had to be told in so many words
had to have the word
thrust in our faces
stuffed in our mouths

iv
Not the speech of clods or crops
and commons, charms for warts,
the tough gutturals of Middle Dutch
in which ons geestelijk erf took root
een ghebreken swelling into een ghebruken
the lack becoming a sudden richness
as the brogue of Hadewijch broke

into songs of searing love in the garden
of Rodeklooster, possessed her god
mouth in mouth, heart in heart, body
in body – that touch of love you could read
as the Brabant liking for what can be rubbed
between finger and thumb appreciatively like soil
or cloth or coin, the currency of the living.

Not for Christina de Wonderbare the plain talk
of her ain folk, her mother's tongue (that dead voice
in her head): she had to go ten better, conjugating
like mad in the lingua franca of kings and bishops
trumpeting her psalms like a tuba mirum
spargens sonum on the cringing air –
to her sisters it was as teasing as backslang:
dologo youlougou geleget whalalgat
lligi alagam salagayiliging? Latin
was how Pater Noster spoke, His
verbums did as they were told, objects
on their best behaviour, marching
to a drumbeat rum bum dorum dum.
His lingo never lapsed. His sentences
got carved in stone. Did she ever fly again,
that necklace of boulders around her?

Her body was so subtle and light that she would walk on any dizzy height or precipice, and hang suspended like a sparrow from the topmost twigs of the loftiest trees. She would take refuge in the tops of trees, the summits of towers or churches, or the roof of any other high building when she wished to pray…

Corpus eius tantae subtilitatis et levitatis erat ut in arduis et sublimibus ambularet et instar passeris in subtilissimis arborum ramusculis dependeret. Cum orare vellet in summitatibus arborum vel turrium vel quarumlibet rerum sublimium fugere cogebatur…

—*Acta Sanctorum* [Acts of the Saints] 2, 15

Up here

Here am I, little jumping Joan.
When nobody's with me, I'm all alone.

Back from the town of the dead, from the house
of my parents, I'm up here making maps, higher and higher,
the power of memory, archaeopteryx, the eye of God.

I'm taking account of the space between rivers
and paths I have taken, recording the length
of the dusk, of things we don't know, of the roads,
the battalions, the ghosts of the Romans, the coast.

Up here you can see for ever, time flying,
the Angel of Mons cast ashore on a tide that is waiting
for no-one. I'm praying that if I come back it'll be as a stitch
in a sail of starlings, a note in the swarming of bees,

frail and fast as the line between languages,
the border unmarked between your life and my life,
today and tomorrow, the quick and the dead.
two chimney pots, bayed windows,
the green door in between them
and lemon-daubed brickwork, smutted now;
it blanks me, close up, appears to hide
behind those images.

Its grey net curtains and metal-stud door,
steep roof-slope, lemon brick, what's behind?
I've never seen anyone enter or leave,
just looking, on the way to work.
In gravel pit lodge, as was,
not a thing's astir.

Past crescent shops where the trams would turn,
stood forward of the building line
it's hidden from package holiday vistas,
spectacular bank accounts, high definition
pay-as-you-watch-them franchise wars …
weekend supplement pages!

That cottage concealed behind Decaux hoardings
has a yard screened by their dark side.
After working, I think you'll find,
here in the shadow of a bigged-up world,
unearned, though it seems to hide
like rain-smell coming from an overcoat,
the actual imagined.

Futurist

'The danseuse must form a continual palpitation of blue veils…
On her chest, like a flower, a large celluloid propeller… she will shake
a sign printed in red: 300 meters – 3 spins – climb… The danseuse
will heap up a lot of green cloth to simulate a green mountain,
and then will leap over it…'
—Marinetti, *Sketch for Dance of the Aviatrix*

I've built my device
    from scratch, from
      a fever of bridges
        between one world
          and the next, I've
            assembled my ribs
              as fuselage, I've danced
                so long on my steel toes
                  that the air's become tense
                and violet as thought,
              the bones of my insteps
            tender as wires. Time
          flies, the horizon swoops
        towards me like a view
      of the century seen
    through glass, full of
splendour and revolt.

All I have to do is
   breathe in and whisk off
      I'm young and weightless
         and unscared of heights
            not part of the old plot
               – the people down there
                  my startled spectators Paris
                     Brussels Milan New York
                        always wrong time wrong place
                     – my engines are intimate
                  and frenzied, *ma machine*
               is à plaisir, my licence to
            perform, I'm vaporised
         by love, lucy in the sky,
      luce intellettual, leaping
   over mountains, running
on empty, leaving it all

behind.

Most mediaeval people differed from most of us today in believing, or at least in being constantly exposed to the belief, that their world stood close to the edge of time.

—R.E. Lerner, *The Powers of Prophecy* (1983)

[Christina] foretold that the Holy Land of Jerusalem would be overcome by the infidel Saracens a long time before it happened. And when the day came on which Jerusalem – along with the Lord's burial place and the Cross of Christ – was captured by Saladin, king of the Persians, she was in Loewen and knew in her heart that the event had come to pass. Thereupon she gave a great cry of triumph; those who were present asked her to explain the reason for this. She said, It is right that I should exult, because today the Lord Christ with his angels is full of rejoicing and exultation: he has made this the occasion on which the whole human race shall be saved.

Sed & multo ante tempore praedixit, quod terra Sancta Jerusalem Saracenis impiis subderetur. Cumque venisset dies, quo a Solahadino, rege Persarum, capta fuit Jerusalem, cum sepulchro Domini & Cruce Christi, ipsa in castro Loen posita, rei eventum cognovit in spiritu. In quo facto vehementer exultans, rogabatur a praesentibus causam tantae exultationis edisserere. Recte, inquit, exulto, quia Christus Dominus hodie cum angelis laetabundus exultans occasionem dedit, qua humani generis multitudo salvetur.

—*Acta Sanctorum* [Acts of the Saints] 3, 32

From Christina's sister to her husband

Luc was away with the Norman army in the north of Spain fighting to repel the Muslim conquerors of the peninsula

What is
my eucharist?

To sip
my God
from off your lips

for my soul
to be wafers
in your mouth

to be born
again the moth's
disciple

flirting
with the hot bright
bare sacraments

that make us
angels

ash

sleeping
palm to palm
in the fragile
afternoon

and undutifully
at night
with tongues

my husband

To Christina from her sister

I lay awake listening to
the wasps rasping
in the roof space,
making papier mache
of the softened rafters.
I thought the roof
would fall in on me. That
my brains would be crushed
by my skull. I dreamt
your breasts were
huge lewd fruit,
that you danced.

I always know when
you are coming back.
When my papers are tidy,
my thoughts subtly ordered,
like yesterday afternoon
as the rain was making perfect
interlocking circles on the pond
and I watched the rounds
widen and complicate themselves
and dissolve into each other
without stopping
– and then the air instead
of freshening grew heavy.
I kept looking over my shoulder
as if I expected you.

What I have is words:
each precise reflective globe
that revolves its own piece
of the seeable world
within a single eye.
When we were together
I'd show off at meal times
constructing sentences long as paragraphs

demanding you define your terms
happiest when I could make you
argue. It always ended in tears,
yours there and then
as you flung away your chair saying
you hated my big-sister games,
mine in secret later.

But the world was yours really
you knew its secret, you flowed
through its density, you felt where
it hurt or was wrong. Your passion
would heal it. God, how you terrified me.
I used to count out words like beads
to get myself to sleep, afraid you'd
fly at me down the chimney.

This morning the garden was still
and potent as if something dangerous
had entered. The waterlogged grass
and tangled vines were heavy
with green flesh, more real than
the snails or wrens that creep in them.

I know you're about to visit again.
I can still see your sweat-stained frock
and your spiralling hair, I was there
when you wanted to die, when you
wanted to kill me.

Don't ever say you
won't come back.

Salvation as a diving-suit

The opera of her breathing fills the whole village
and even on the hillside they can hear her enlightenment
bubbling like a hash-pipe in the mouth of God.

From inside the helmet she watches the others swim.
Shoals of bishops and other big fish nose at the glass
manifesting the dark markings of their consciences.

Saved for sure, she has to be weighted down to the sea-bed
of the market square. But sinning's smell seeps in at the seams,
a slow inundation of children's hair and used bank notes.

Her visor is cloudy with what she knows – she reels up to the light,
to the air that is promised, the top of the towers of silence,
the blue, the sky, the burial. Walking in space.

What goes around

'The natural condition of our existence is to revolve'
—Mevlana Jalaluddin Rumi

I
am
the
great E
the electron
and the ecstacy
I am MC^2 meaning
mistress of ceremonies
I'm a spinning top, a prayer- or
potter's wheel, I'm the RotoGyrator
at the fair your Catherine can't get enough of
tomorrow's anticyclone over the Irish Sea
I invented the roulette the boomerang
the spindle for pricking fingers
see how the butter thickens
and how I chase my tail
without getting dizzy
the still centre
my favourite
show
am
I

How Saint Christina sang

'Then she stopped spinning and sang. No-one could imitate
the sounds that came from deep in her chest nor make sense
of the syllables; no breath came out of her nose or mouth,
but it was like angels singing'
—Thomas de Chantimpré

think of it like a Mongolian trance-chant
sung on the bottomless in-breath
like a journey along the silk road
being rolled back past the dust-heaps
and broken walls of frontier towns, back
past the one remaining window made
of a slice of lapis lazuli and the still wind-chimes
back into the rib-cage, the swaddle, the chrysalis

or find in your mind an Inuit song
sung by one by two by sister-twins
like the ice-night and the eery not-sun lights
hologramming on the sky's retina
breathing down each other's wind-pipes
the in-out of the ice-sheet across the eyelids
the sound-harpoon in the blank ice-pool

see, she does not cloud the mirror

The cave

They have rolled back the stone and gathered like doctors to nose
at the mouth of my cave. In here there are scores of us, some
from an earlier time and others like angels or crows

who have yet to arrive. They are waiting for me to come
to myself while I lie here and dream that I'm flying, down backroads
and bypasses, shortcuts and cinder tracks, sailing offshore

past islands there's no calling in at, past stations and crossroads,
the small roads which line up and ask to be taken somewhere.
The doctors are patiently waiting and watching this brief

middle passage of speaking in songs which I reel out behind me,
hoping that one of them catches my thread or the drift
that is piling like letters unanswered outside the window

gathering weight like a feather or mirror held to the lips
heavy as firewood or water brought home on the hip.

When I woke, the darkest dreams continued… I was forced to travel

'…levé, je continuais les rêves les plus tristes…
Je dus voyager…'
—Rimbaud, *Une saison en enfer*

There's a face I see in the wells, sits
like a crow on my shoulder. Home-sick
and sick of home, these small fires
I tread – the way these strangers
build their walls, and the unfamiliar flies.

Stopping to sleep, I dream the bare song
under my heels: of the rising before dawn,
the ashes dead in the grate, and the town
rolling away at my feet. In the morning,
the black trees have vanished from the field.

I walk the dry hand of the earth and in that oven
burn away my name and the place that I was born.

After this, she left her home and family, and made for the town of Loewen near the German border. And here she spent nine years with Jutta, a recluse of the greatest religious devotion. God was surely working wonders through her. Actually, it was from this recluse that I learnt much of what I have written about Christina – I made the long journey from my part of France on that account.

Post haec de domo propria & cognatione digressa, castrum in confinio Alamanniae, quod Loen dicitur, expetivit: ubi cum quadam religiosissimae vitae reclusa Ivetta nomine, moram per novennium faciens, mira per eam operatus est Dominus. A qua reclusa, multa, quae de Christina scripsi, revelata suscepi: de longinquis enim Galliarum partibus ad eam propter hoc veni.

—*Acta Sanctorum* [Acts of the Saints] 4, 38

Virgin

'To choose virginity is to assert one's independence from the insistence of nature – virginity is the repudiation of determinism.'
—Howard Barker, programme notes for *Ursula: Fear of the estuary*

These soft brown wallflowers
smell thick and sweet as pigs
while spring's open throat
sucks at me like a lover
a greedy child
that I refuse, I refuse.

Chastity contains me like a rind or chalice
I am an angel's eye containing the seven gates of light
Gonging apes and blaring asses are contained by this flimsy trellis.
A wrenling's feather could contain ten times my soul's full weight.

I've heard the crocodile will survive
long after the last man
has wept for the last woman
the crocodile who in civil war
when no one comes to throw meat
can go for a year without eating
has never asked for love.

Desire divides me like a sword or dance
I am logic's razor dividing the atom from itself
Gnats and mastodons are divided by improbabilities of chance
An iota could divide a thousand surds from the one thing said.

Here's a sachet of corn
pinned to a letter, suddenly
spilling like golden rain
on the learned doctor's table.

The grain pours every month
from the breasts of a young farm-girl
in full flower anno domini 1785.
In 1993 a statue lets down her tears
to a teenager in black stockings.
I am intact after all this time
I am an archive of all appetites
I am your story of survival
against the odds
against nature
I refuse explanations
I do not ask for love.

Letter from Hadewijch

Ah, dear child, may God give you what my heart desires for you, and may you love Him as He deserves…

From the age of ten I have been overwhelmed with such passionate love that I would have died during the first two years of this experience if God had not granted me a power unknown to common people and made me recover with his own being… I was aware of many signs that were between him and me, as with friends who are used to concealing little and revealing much when their feelings for each other have grown most intimate, when they taste, eat, and drink and consume each other wholly. Through these many signs God, my lover, showed to me early in life, He made me gain much confidence in Him and I often thought that no one loved Him as dearly as I…

—Hadewijch of Brabant, poet and mystic (13th-c.CE)

What the poet said

Perhaps there's another way of phrasing it,
life, death and the whole damn thing,
language as a way of learning how to lose:
'like forest leaves falling in the first chill
of autumn, like birds flocking to leave
the cold year and go south over the sea,
so the dead souls jostled at the water's edge,
their hands outstretched towards the other –
always the other – shore, yearning to be first.'
Sunt lacrimae rerum yes and this sadness
at the heart of things the master-poet made
a twelve-part pagan epic of seems easier
to bear these days than raptures of rebirth,
exaltations of suffering. To be touched by
the finity of. Not to try to fill the void with.

Besides this vertigo of stone I wait
like an animal for the rain to stop.
Offer lips, nails, blue as Mary.

The lichen drips, hanging on
for a dear sort of life and I hear them,
the widows, say *Why did it have to be her.*

We shall have no clouds today, only
the wasps' slow eclipse of the windfalls
and archangel heron, fanning what fires?

Bone by bone I lay myself out
in the grass, wonder what will you do
to put the heart across me now.

The mountain is paralysed, and she
is on it, riding the dark and what's left
of the up-swing, the funfair, the planets.

Down in the village, several of the men
are searching for their oxen. And how
will it be if she never speaks again?

Take it or leave it. The butcher's dog
and the boiling vat of bones. Impossible.
And not one of them glad to see me back.

Then last night it came to me like a wolf
to a small town at midnight. The smell of Jonah
so long in the whale, of wake-food wasted.

Alone in night's wide bed, I spill over
into the dawn and the private life of birds.
The day heats up. The young men come,

the apple-pickers and sieve-makers.
When I am gone, will they divide my body
up or place me on anyone's tongue?

The last years of her life Christina passed in the convent of St. Catherine at Saint-Trond [Sint-Truiden], and there she died at the age of seventy-four. Even while she lived there were some who regarded her with great respect. Louis, Count of Looz, treated her as a friend, welcoming her to his castle, accepting her rebukes, and on his deathbed insisting on manifesting his conscience to her. Blessed Mary of Oignies had regard for her, the prioress of St. Catherine's praised her obedience and St. Lutgardis sought her advice.

—A. Butler, *Lives of the Saints* (1756–9)

She settles down after her miraculous time as a bird

I woke up heavier than the day before, I could feel
my brain's weight on the pillow, the lead in my heels.
Perhaps I only think I remember the girlish appeal
of being heaven-bent, a feather on the breath of God.

I do not find glory easy any more, the ifs and buts
intrude, a buzzing in my spirit's ears. Or has He shut
Himself away? The stairs I climb go down not up.
I've forgotten how the sparrow does it, the shooting star.

So am I earthed, at last, catchable? Caught?
Who or what was I flying from? I thought
it was you, your body, your badness. I ought
to have known. This is where the mystery starts.

From the Prioress' journal

I have caught her again, crooning like a sick goose
at the stones in the atrium, 'I know and am this house'.

In chapel I see her perched, listening to the wings of the moths
quivering behind the tight needlework of the altarcloth

and I know that she's flying again, that the dusty rood-screen
is a mirador, the font a fountain in some other Christ's harem

where she and the moon together go naked in the night
under their black robes, their small breasts silent and white,

their miraculous markings and silver anklets hidden till
they fall to lie cooling in marble pools, shameless and still.

These dark days I watch her in the refectory, pecking
at her food, one eye on the small high windows, working

out the distance, there and back again, our winter visitant.
In the tallow smoke her eye glitters with that other continent.

The visit

[When Christina was a girl] Christ… gave her the grace of inner peace and often came to her from heaven's secret places. But she kept this to herself: indeed, the more she became familiar with God, the more secretive she was.
—Thomas de Chantimpré

The day we made the walk to Brusthem was the tail end of a summer
storm, the sky sagged low over the parish's flats and tracks,
whole limbs of sweet chestnut shambled on the grass –
at the top end of the allotments where you can see down over
a score of neat roofs the others waited for me to catch up;
we leaned on our sticks trying to find the past and the tree
where we skipped and giddied about till we lost our breath
and flung ourselves down on the spot and the old biddies tutted
that we'd scared away the fairies. Looking north between here and
the church you can see the light turn green as if the air's been stained
by weeping-willow, trefoil, wild iris – a verdure breathed by the
    landscape.
I didn't always see these things. Now, I walk more slowly.
I was still catching my breath, and waved Beatrix and the others
    to go on.
My mother knew the names and sympathies of all the plants –
    toothache, cramp,
bad dreams, the ones you wake sick and shrieking from.
My sisters used to grumble, tease, Shut up it's only the devil
    paying a visit.
I was tired that afternoon, the walk was further than I remembered,
my small pilgrimage. I wasn't sure for a moment who was there,
    I heard my name,
I thought – like playing hide-and-seek. But something used to
    happen to me, yes,
I'd stand in the field with my secret, it was my secret; and then the
    others would moan

But we can see you, stupid! They'd drag me off to church
   or the milking.
My name, I was sure heard my name. It was just that kind
   of afternoon,
the sky rinsed now and vacant, everything in waiting, stilled,
clear as stoup water. Perhaps, who knows, I lost consciousness
   for a second
standing there. There are many explanations. To be touched,
   to be visited –
it's what we all want. The unrecognised figure on the path.
   Our name called.

Calling on Christ, Christina breathed her last... Then Beatrix... flung herself on the body of the deceased, crying out over the body of the deceased and wailing bitterly. And between her cries she asked the dead one again and again why she had left and gone to God. Then – O wonderful to tell! – before much time had passed, as Beatrix was sobbing in the poor dead ears, Christina returned to her body, heaved a deep sigh and with anxious gaze said in a loud voice to the one calling her back: O Beatrix, why have your disturbed me? Why have you called me back? I was being escorted onward into the sight of Christ; but now, sister, quickly put the question you have to ask and let me go back, I beg you, to where I wish to be, with God. Then did Beatrix ask what was on her mind, and so received her reply...

Vocante Christo, Christina spiritum exhalavit... Tunc Beatrix... ruit super defunctae corpus, clamans susper defunctae corpus, et ejaculans vehementer. Cumque inter clamandum defunctam saepius interrogaret... cur... abisset ad Dominum... Mira res! mox ubi Beatrix mortuis auribus inclamavit, Christina reversa ad corpus, grave suspirium edidit anxioque vultu revocantem reverberans dixit: O Beatrix! quid me inquietastie? Quare revocasti me? Iam exhibenda ducebar ad conspectum Christi; sed nunc soror mi, quid vis, festinanter interroga et sinas me, obsecro, ad Domini concupita reverti. Tunc Beatrix quod proponebat interrogans, responsum ab illa recepit...

—*Acta Sanctorum* [Acts of the Saints] 5, 52

The tunnel

Ask me what it was like at the end of the tunnel,
if it was white as a moon-surgeon's fingernail,
light as the water out from the crush of the wheel,
as the breast of an owl, too white to enter,
too tight a fit at the lych gate almost,
then there you are, a bride in the garden at Sissinghurst,
up at the summit of Everest, not one step further
to go, white as the snowfall of morphine,
the chalky descent to the house you were born in,
a sheet, a broken back mended, the third day, or roses?

Or was it black, another dark tunnel
crammed in the arse or mouth of the first,
your very own mine-shaft or mad-house of lost
without trace, of no face left on the shroud
to speak or talk about, black as the bite
the earth takes out of the moon, as the axefall
of slurry, as a mouthful of silence, the heart
of the slag-heap, as hungry, as no chance,
as no hope of getting a word out,
as your own name forgotten, as eaten already?

Christina died in the convent in 1224. Twenty-five years later, a strange lady in white appeared and told the abbess that the nuns should wash the bones and show them to the people. And a lot of miracles began to happen there…

In the 18th century King Johann Wilhelm von Balz-Neuberg had a great admiration for Christina and wanted a piece of her forearm. In exchange he gave a solid gold monstrance worth 57,000 golden florins. You have to realise what value that little piece of bone had for him – relics opened the gate to eternal life…

— Danny Gennez, municipal guide, Sint-Truiden (1996)

Relic

Who could stab a finger at the chest
of her childhood and say, that was the day
it arrived in the village, the stuff with X-ray eyes,
settling itself in the easy chair of her flesh,
sacred sternum, solar plexus, her future, her stars.

Worth more than gold or gems, this radiation,
spirit of the knee-cap and the finger-bone
swung like an ammeter or steeple vane in the lap
of the wind, only one place to go from here,
walking on water, dancing through fire, the next step.

The King of Portugal has her finger. Wing-tip, grounded.
Shrine to the immortal possibilities of vertebrates.
Inside the trunk or chest the bones glow in the dark,
not wanted on voyage. The patellae of penitence,
the ulna and radius of flight, these are her only children.

And will our daughters fly?

'Certainly she ran very great risks In passing over savage countries'
— *The Manchester Guardian,* reporting Amy Johnson's solo flight
from London to Australia

We had hollow bones, learnt to fly
early on rice-paper wings of
mental arithmetic, of words
like idiosyncrasy, infinity.
We were earthed, of course, and now
in my dreams I cling to unhinged
ladders that tremble over the abyss
as if I had never surfed the Milky Way
with the angel's heel as compass.

Those women who rode helmeted
like Athene in their burnished Lockheeds
and De Havillands in the curled clouds
– Amy, Amelia, the names of love –
carried the thermoses of soup and studied
the effects of prolonged flight
on the human body. Their solitary flesh
fell like melted wax into the waves,

their beautiful engines burst in a flimsy
of mothwing and sparrow-bone. But
they bore the names of love, they knew
the necessity of flight. Didn't Christina
say her prayers hanging by her heels
in the tree-tops? She's a high-wire walker
for God, a holy aerialiste, a bird, a bird!

The owl is wise, is death
The pelican is holy, the dove desire.
The vulture is divine, the swans
are our daughters' brothers
sewn up in a shirt: on the north wind

shall they fly, like ships of fury.
The lapwing guards the name of god,
secret agent to King Solomon himself.

She is pure deceit, peewit peewit
you cannot take her by surprise.

And what of the lark hauled up up
into the sky's rafters on a thread
of adoration, a solitary majestic
tongue, a meteor falling
towards the stars, a synonym
of bliss? Oh how you flew,
Christina, and how we envied!

We stroke our daughters' lengthening backs
where the bones are sprouting –
let them not feel as theirs
the dutifulness of geese
the sadness of the cassowary.

References

pp. xi and 61: *Butler's Lives of the Saints,* ed. Thurston and Attwater, Volume III, 1956.

pp. xii and 15: Herbert Thurston 'The transition period of Catholic mysticism', *The Month*, August 1922.

p. xii: James Bentley *A Calendar of Saints.* Orbis, 1986.

p. xiii: Caroline Walker Bynum, *Holy Feast, Holy Fast: The Religious Significance of Food to Mediaeval Women*. University of California Press, 1987.

p. 2: Tertullian, Church Father, quoted in Walter Vandereycken and Ron van Deth *From Fasting Girls to Anorexic Saints: The History of Self-Starvation.* Athlone Press, 1994.

p. 4: Poem by Radbod, Bishop of Utrecht, tenth century.

p. 8: Poem by Paulinus of Nola, consul and scholar, fifth century.

p. 9: extracts from Burchard of Worms's *Corrector,* quoted in John Shinners (ed.), *Mediaeval Popular Religion*, *1000–1500.* Broadview Press, 1997.

p. 18: Poem by Siegebert of Gembloux (d. 1112): an elegy for the legendary 10,000 virgin martyrs who accompanied Saint Ursula as she travelled down the Rhine to break off her betrothal to an eminent prince. They were all put to death.

p. 24: MS. of Benediktbeuern, No.158 of the so-called *Carmina Burana,* a thirteenth-century collection of anonymous complaints on fortune, recruiting verses for the Crusades, drinking songs and love lyrics.

p. 27: John Shinners (ed.) *Mediaeval Popular Religion*, *1000–1500*. Broadview Press, 1997.

p. 31: From *O ignis Spiritus Paracliti,* one of the nine sequentiae composed by Hildegard von Bingen

p. 36: Robert E. Lerner *The Powers of Prophecy: the Cedar of Lebanon Vision from the Mongol Onslaught to the Dawn of the Enlightenment.* University of California Press, 1983.

p. 53: transl. Ria Vanderauwera 'The Brabant mystic: Hadewijch', in Katharina M. Wilson (ed.) *Mediaeval Women Writers.* Manchester University Press, 1984.

p. 69: Personal commentary by Danny Gennez, municipal guide in Sint-Truiden.

All the mediaeval Latin poems appear in Helen Waddell's *Mediaeval Latin Lyrics* Constable and Co. Ltd., 1938, but these translations were made by Lesley Saunders.

All other extracts are from the *Acta Sanctorum*, an encyclopaedic text organised according to each saint's feast day); the extracts selected here have been translated by Lesley Saunders, except for the first and second extracts, which appear in Butler.

Two Rivers Press has been publishing in and about Reading
since 1994. Founded by the artist Peter Hay (1951–2003),
the press continues to delight readers, local and further afield,
with its varied list of individually designed,
thought-provoking books.